Who is Jesus?

W M Henry and Michael Penny

ISBN: 978-1-78364-464-3

**The Open Bible Trust
Fordland Mount, Upper Basildon,
Reading, RG8 8LU, UK.**

www.obt.org.uk

Who is Jesus?

Contents

Page

Jesus!
Who is He?

Jesus! Who is He?

Many people today are interested in public opinion, from pop-stars to politicians. Thus we have pop-charts and public opinion polls. Our Lord also expressed an interest in knowing what people thought of Him for when He came to the region of Caesarea Philippi He asked His disciples, "Who do people say the Son of Man is?" (Matthew 16:13). The answers were varied. The disciples replied, "Some say John the Baptist; others say Elijah; and still others, Jeremiah or one of the prophets."

- John the Baptist
- Elijah
- Jeremiah
- One of the prophets

John the Baptist

It may seem strange to us that any should think the Lord Jesus to be John the Baptist but they were related, through Mary and Elizabeth, and there may have been some physical, family resemblance. However, some, possibly much, of what they said and did was the same. For example:

- Both opened their ministry with the words "Repent, for the kingdom of heaven is near." (Matthew 3:1; 4:17)
- Both were associated with baptism. (John 1:25-27; John 3:22-23; John 4:1-2)
- Both upheld the Law of Moses. (Matthew 14:2-4; 5:17-19)

However, it still seems strange that people thought Jesus to be John. By this time John had been dead for a little while, but it seems that Herod, himself, may have been responsible for the view that Jesus was John.

At that time Herod the tetrarch heard the reports about Jesus, and he said to his attendants, "This is John the Baptist; he has risen from the dead! That is why miraculous powers are at work in him." (Matthew 14:1-2)

Elijah

This view, that the Lord Jesus is Elijah, is not the least bit strange. It is very understandable.

The last prophet sent to Israel was Malachi, and his words close our Old Testament.

> "See, I will send my messenger, who will prepare the way before me. Then suddenly the Lord you are seeking will come to his temple; the messenger of the covenant, whom you desire, will come," says the Lord Almighty. (Malachi 3:1)

> "See, I will send you the prophet Elijah before that great and dreadful day of the Lord comes. He will turn the hearts of the

fathers to their children, and the hearts of the children to their fathers; or else I will come and strike the land with a curse." (Malachi 4:5-6)

Thus the last statement from God to the people of Israel in Old Testament times was that there was to be a messenger who would prepare the way for Him. That Elijah was to come before the great and dreadful day of the Lord.

It is not surprising then that some Jews thought John the Baptist to be Elijah (John 1:20-25), and neither is it surprising that some thought the Lord Jesus to be Elijah. Even today, at some of their religious celebrations, some Jews place an empty chair at the table, in case Elijah comes.[1]

Jeremiah

As well as having their Scriptures, our Old Testament, the Jews of Christ's day also had

---

[1] For more on the differences of these two statements in Malachi see *Elijah and John the Baptist* by Michael Penny, published by the Open Bible Trust.

what many call the Apocrypha. They also possessed various other non-canonical books such as *The Assumption of Moses* and *The Book of Enoch*, alluded to in the letter of Jude.

Two books in the Apocrypha refer to Jeremiah. 2 Maccabees 2:1-12 states that before the Babylonian Exile, Jeremiah took the tent, the Ark of the Covenant and the altar of incense out of the Temple and hid them in a cave in Mount Nebo[2].

2 Esdras 2:18 states, "I will send you help, my servants Isaiah and Jeremiah", and some Jews believed that before the coming of the Messiah Jeremiah would return, recover the ark and the altar of incense and the glory of God would once more come upon the people again.

In stating that Jesus was Elijah or Jeremiah, the people of that day were giving Him high honour, for Elijah and Jeremiah were the expected

---

[2] Jeremiah is also mentioned in 2 Maccabees 15:1-14.

forerunners, and when they arrived, the Messiah and the kingdom would shortly follow.

One of the Prophets

This answer is also understandable. John the Baptist was looked upon by the people as a prophet from God, and Christ gave him that status also (Matthew 11:9-13; 14:5). Jesus applied the word to Himself and the people saw Him as "the prophet from Nazareth in Galilee" (Matthew 13:57; 21:11). People could see what He was doing was different, and that this made Him different (note Nicodemus' words in John 3:2).

However, seeing Jesus as 'a' prophet, as 'one' of the prophets, is an incomplete truth. He was more than 'a' prophet; He was 'the' prophet like Moses. Moses was the major prophet spoken of in the Old Testament, and Jesus is 'the' prophet of the New Testament and He fulfilled a major prophecy given to Moses in Deuteronomy 18:15-19

The Lord your God will raise up for you *a prophet like me* from among your own brothers. You must listen to him. For this is what you asked of the Lord your God at Horeb on the day of the assembly when you said, "Let us not hear the voice of the Lord our God nor see this great fire anymore, or we will die."

The Lord said to me: "What they say is good. I will raise up for them *a prophet like you* from among their brothers; I will put my words in his mouth, and he will tell them everything I command him. If anyone does not listen to my words that **the** prophet speaks in my name, I myself will call him to account.

Peter spoke of this in Acts 3:22-23:

"For Moses said, 'The Lord your God will raise up for you a prophet like me from among your own people; you must listen to everything he tells you. Anyone who does not listen to him will be completely cut off from among his people.'"

Today

However, if our Lord asked us the same question as He asked the disciples, I wonder what answers we would give. Who do people, today, the non-Christian general population, say that Jesus is?

- A myth: He never existed.
- He's a man, He's just a man.
- The husband of Mary Magdalene.
- One of the wisest of men.
- A prophet, just like Mohammed or Buddha.

A myth: He never existed

It is quite amazing that some think Jesus of Nazareth never existed, yet the evidence for Him being on this planet is far greater than that for Julius Caesar! Non-biblical historical evidence for the existence of Christ is given in *Did Jesus of Nazareth actually exist?* which is available as a free download from **www.obt.org.uk** .

He's a man, He's just a man

Well He certainly was a man, but He was not 'just a man'. These words come from the refrain of the song *I don't know how to love Him* sung by Mary Magdalene in the musical *Jesus Christ: Superstar*. They echo the thinking of many who see Jesus as mere man, no more than 'one of us'. True! He was man (Hebrews 2:14-18), but He was much more.

The husband of Mary Magdalene

The love displayed by the fictional Mary Magdalene in *Jesus Christ: Superstar* becomes marriage in *The Da Vinci Code*. However, there is not the slightest historical evidence for this and if Jesus had been married to Mary Magdalene we would have had a different scenario in His dying moments.

> Near the cross of Jesus stood his mother, his mother's sister, Mary the wife of Clopas, and Mary Magdalene. When Jesus saw his mother there, and the disciple

whom he loved standing nearby, he said to his mother, "Dear woman, here is your son," and to the disciple, "Here is your mother." From that time on, this disciple took her into his home. (John 19:25-27)

Here we see the Lord putting his mother Mary into the care of John, but if He had been married to Mary Magdalene, he would, first of all, have taken care of her needs and given John the responsibility of looking after her. The wife takes precedence over the mother, as Christ Himself showed by His words in Matthew 19:4-6:

"Haven't you read," he replied, "that at the beginning the Creator 'made them male and female,' and said, 'For this reason a man will leave his father and mother and be united to his wife, and the two will become one flesh'? So they are no longer two, but one. Therefore what God has joined together, let man not separate."

One of the wisest of men

In his book *The Greatest Thinkers*, Edward De Bono lists Jesus, but who else is in that list? We have such people as:

> Moses, Plato, Aristotle, Augustine, Copernicus, Luther, Newton and Einstein.

But we also have people like:
> Kant, Darwin, Marx, Freud and Sartre.

Is Jesus just like any of these?

A prophet like Mohammed or Buddha

One of the 'politically correct' positions in today's society is to reckon all religions to be equally valid paths to God. Thus their founders must all have equal status and politically correct people are prone to elevate these founders to the status of prophet, but they refuse to distinguish one from the other. This may suit 'liberal' theology in Islam, Buddhism, Hinduism and Christianity, as it tends to be the liberal theologians who desire some form of religious unity amongst all faiths. Also, as their views are the main ones, almost exclusive ones, heard in the British media, it is not surprising that much of public opinion in Britain sees little difference between Jesus and Mohammed or Buddha.

But back to the Bible

Having heard the disciples tell Him who other people thought Him to be, the Lord next turned to the disciples, looked at them, and said:

> "But what about you? …..Who do you say I am?" (Matthew 16:15)

Peter replied:

> "You are the Christ, the Son of the living God." (Matthew 16:16)

Which brought this acclamation from the Lord:

"Blessed are you, Simon son of Jonah, for this was not revealed to you by man, but by my Father in heaven."

However, we would be wrong to think that this was suddenly revealed to Peter for earlier, when Christ saved them from the storm at sea, and Peter wanted to walk on the water just like Him, we read:

> Then Peter got down out of the boat, walked on the water and came towards Jesus. But when he saw the wind, he was afraid and, beginning to sink, cried out, "Lord, save me!" Immediately Jesus reached out his hand and caught him. "You of little faith," he said, "why did you doubt?" And when they climbed into the boat, the wind died down. Then those who were in the boat worshipped him, saying, "Truly you are the Son of God." (Matthew 14:29-33)

However, what did Peter mean by 'the Christ' and 'the Son of the living God'?

Jesus:
The Christ

Jesus:
The Christ

A twin title

Peter's great confession of the Lord Jesus in Matthew 16:16 is an important point in the Lord's ministry. The Lord's commendation of Peter shows the accuracy of his response, but also indicates that it was God the Father who had revealed the truth to him. However, what did Peter mean by the two aspects to the title?

- The Christ and
- The Son of the living God

The apostle John structured his gospel around a series of signs that Jesus performed during His time on earth and towards the end of the gospel he says:

> Jesus did many other miraculous signs in the presence of his disciples, which are

not recorded in this book. But these are written that you may believe that Jesus is the Christ, the Son of God, and that by believing you may have life in his name. (John 20:30-31)

Again we can see the double title: the Christ; the Son of God. There were these two aspects to the Lord Jesus' identity and the functions He fulfilled.

In the next two sections of this booklet we shall consider John's presentation of Jesus as the Christ and as the Son of God, respectively.

The Christ – The Old Testament Presentation

The title 'Christ' or 'Messiah' means 'The anointed one' and He is described by the New Bible Dictionary as 'the central figure of expectation in the Jewish religion.' There are a number of aspects of His character and activity in the Old Testament and it is helpful to see how these expectations were fulfilled in Jesus.

He will perform signs and wonders

In Isaiah 35:3-6 we read:

> Strengthen the feeble hands, steady the knees that give way; say to those with fearful hearts, "Be strong, do not fear; your God will come, he will come with vengeance; with divine retribution he will come to save you." Then will the eyes of the blind be opened and the ears of the deaf unstopped. Then will the lame leap like a deer, and the mute tongue shout for joy. Water will gush forth in the wilderness and streams in the desert.

The context of this passage is the Lord's intervention in human affairs in the form of Messiah and the delivery and restoration of Israel. This was why the Lord performed the signs and wonders that He did – miracles of all types – over disease, over the forces of nature. They were the credentials by which He revealed Himself to Israel. The passage in Isaiah links the miraculous signs with 'vengeance' and 'divine retribution.' However, neither of these elements were a part of the Lord's *first* advent, but they will be very much a feature of His *second* coming.

We can also see the deferral of the day of vengeance in the incident where Jesus stood up to read the Scriptures in the synagogue at Nazareth. The reading was also from the book of Isaiah:

> The Spirit of the Lord is on me, because he has anointed me to preach good news to the poor. He has sent me to proclaim freedom for the prisoners and recovery of sight for the blind, to release the oppressed, to proclaim the year of the Lord's favour. (Luke 4:18-19)

Luke tells us that 'the eyes of everyone in the synagogue were fastened on him.' No wonder. He stopped in the middle of the passage. Isaiah 61:1-2, from where the reading was taken goes on to say '…and the day of vengeance of our God.' However, that day had not yet arrived and, having omitted reference to it the Lord went on to say

> Today this Scripture (i.e. speaking of the day of deliverance) is fulfilled in your hearing.

The Messiah of whom Isaiah spoke, who would perform signs and wonders, including the healing of the blind and who would preach a message of deliverance, was standing among them. Sadly, they did not recognise Him for who He was and spoke disparagingly of 'Joseph's son' (Luke 4:22).

He will be a servant who suffers

Isaiah contains a number of sections which speak of Messiah, that are collectively known as the 'servant songs'. Chapters 52-53 of Isaiah contain some of the finest poetry in the Old Testament. In these chapters the prophet describes the suffering of the Lord's servant Messiah. Chapter 53 is well known but the closing verses of chapter 52 set the scene.

See, my servant will act wisely; he will be raised and lifted up and highly exalted. Just as there were many who were appalled at him – his appearance was so disfigured beyond that of any man and his form marred beyond human likeness – so he will sprinkle many nations. (Isaiah 52:13-15)

Chapter 53 makes it clear that the suffering of Messiah is not on His own behalf – it is for others. His sacrifice is for our benefit, to bring us healing.

He was pierced for our transgressions, he was crushed for our iniquities; the punishment that brought us peace was upon him, and by his wounds we are healed. (Isaiah 53:5)

He will be a servant who rules.

This servant is no helpless victim. Although he does not vaunt Himself, He is destined to be a ruler. Isaiah 42:1-4 tells us:

Here is my servant, whom I uphold, my chosen one in whom I delight; I will put my Spirit on him and he will bring justice to the nations. He will not shout or cry out, or raise his voice in the streets. A bruised reed he will not break, and a smouldering wick he will not snuff out. In faithfulness he will bring forth justice; he will not falter or be discouraged till he establishes justice on earth. In his law the islands will put their hope.

From these verses it can be seen that this is no ordinary servant. He is a servant who is a king and His mission is nothing less than to 'establish justice on the earth.' Isaiah 42 indicates that he will not announce His arrival by drawing attention to Himself. Matthew 12:18-21 applies this prophecy to the Lord Jesus and indicates that the Lord fulfilled it by asking people not to reveal His identity, as He performed signs of healing. He is a servant who is going to rule. He will be in a position to establish universal justice. This is no ordinary servant.

He will deliver Israel and will have dominion over the nations

Given the words of Isaiah 35 quoted above, it is understandable that the Jews believed that their Messiah would be a military leader and on a number of occasions tried to pressgang the Lord Jesus into playing such a role. For example, in John 6:15 after the feeding of the five thousand, the people, excited by the sign they had just witnessed and recognising this as one of the signs of His Messiahship wanted to make Him king by force. He rejected this approach, but a king is what He is, as He confirmed to Pilate in John 18:37.

He will be the Son of David: A King on His throne

This servant has a royal lineage and His destiny is to rule on the throne of His father, David. Isaiah 9 contains familiar words that are quoted in every watch night service at Christmas:

For to us a child is born, to us a son is given, and the government will be on his shoulders. And he will be called Wonderful Counsellor, Mighty God, Everlasting Father, Prince of Peace. Of the increase of his government and peace there will be no end. He will reign on David's throne and over his kingdom, establishing and upholding it with justice and righteousness from that time on and forever. (Isaiah 9:6-7)

These verses again emphasise the justice of His government, but they make it clear that He will be the king of Israel, sitting on the throne of David in perpetuity. In another familiar passage, Micah predicts where Messiah will be born:

But you, Bethlehem Ephrathah, though you are small among the clans of Judah, out of you will come for me one who will rule over Israel, whose origins are from of old, from ancient times. (Micah 5:2)

When the wise men came to Herod, seeking the 'King of the Jews' Herod asked the chief priests and teachers of the law where Christ was to be born. In response, they quoted Micah's prophecy. (Matthew 2:5-6)

He will be the Son of Man

Daniel 7:13-14 contains part of Daniel's vision of the end times, when God will overthrow the evil kingdoms on earth and establish His own kingdom. The One who is to do this is described as 'one like a son of man'.

> There before me was one like a son of man, coming with the clouds of heaven. He approached the Ancient of Days and was led into his presence. He was given authority, glory and sovereign power; all peoples, nations and men of every language worshipped him. His dominion is an everlasting dominion that will not pass away, and his kingdom is one that will never be destroyed.

'Son of Man' is a title that Jesus frequently uses of Himself, to the confusion of the Jews (e.g. see John 12:34). Daniel applies the term to Messiah, who will come with the authority of God Himself, to establish an everlasting kingdom.

The Old Testament picture of Messiah contains some paradoxical elements. He will be a conquering hero who will perform miraculous signs to authenticate His identity, deliver Israel from her enemies and establish a kingdom from His base in Jerusalem, on the throne of His father, David. The kingdom will have worldwide influence. It will be everlasting and will be characterised by justice and truth.

Yet at the same time, Messiah is presented as a servant who will not publicly proclaim Himself. Not only so, but He will suffer and die, not for His own sins but for the sins of others. He will take the sins of the world on Himself and pay the penalty for them.

How can the contradictions be reconciled? One of the problems with Old Testament prophecies is that it is hard to separate the two comings of the Lord Jesus into the world. We, with the benefit of hindsight and the further revelation of God's purposes in the New Testament can see that the deliverance of Israel and the setting up of the kingdom belong to a future coming.

This, then, is a summary of the Old Testament background to Messiah. The next section will explore the way in which John presents the Lord Jesus as Messiah in his gospel.

The Christ – John's presentation

John is a highly skilful writer. He sets out his material selectively, not always sticking to the chronological order of events but grouping discourses, signs and incidents together to suit his purposes. His presentation of Jesus as Messiah can be broadly grouped under four headings:

The reaction of individuals who met Jesus

After John's brief introduction of the Lord in the early verses of chapter 1, he brings onto the stage person after person who encounter Jesus and who immediately recognise Him for who He is. First, John the Baptist warns the priests and Levites that there was One living among them who was of much greater worth than he (verses 26-27). Later in the chapter (verses 29-31) John identifies this One as Jesus:

> Look, the Lamb of God, who takes away the sin of the world! This is the one I meant when I said, 'A man who comes after me has surpassed me because he was before me.' I myself did not know him, but the reason I came baptising with water was that he might be revealed to Israel.

We can see the echoes of Isaiah's 'servant' passages in these words – his description of the suffering servant as being like a lamb led to the slaughter (Isaiah 53:7), a servant who gave up

His life for the sins of others. The identification of Jesus as Messiah was the focal point of John's ministry – the voice crying in the wilderness to make the way ready for the Lord (John 1:23) – is emphasised at the end of verse 31: it is His revelation to Israel.

Andrew, one of John's disciples, heard his master's words and followed Jesus. John 1:39 tells us that he spent the day with Him. We don't know what was discussed but the first thing Andrew does is to seek out his brother Simon:

> "We have found the Messiah (that is, the Christ)." (verse 41)

Andrew was immediately convinced, and introduced his brother Simon to Jesus. We then read of the call of Philip (verse 43). Again John does not tell us what words were exchanged but Philip immediately sought out Nathanael and told him:

We have found the one Moses wrote about in the Law, and about whom the prophets also wrote – Jesus of Nazareth, the son of Joseph (verse 45).

Nathanael's derision about Nazareth was blown away when he was introduced to Jesus.

Rabbi, you are the Son of God; you are the king of Israel. (verse 56)

Here we can see the twin titles – Son of God, but also the One of whom the prophets wrote – Messiah, the king of Israel. Jesus wryly comments that Nathanael believed on the basis of very little, but that he would see much greater proofs of the Lord's identity.

I tell you the truth, you shall see heaven open, and the angels of God ascending and descending on the Son of Man. (verse 51)

Here for the first time the Lord applies the designation of the One in Daniel's vision to Himself.

So in the first chapter of John, we see many echoes of the Old Testament presentation of Messiah – the lamb, the sin-bearer, the king of Israel, the one of whom the prophets spoke, the Son of Man. But, perhaps more importantly, having read the responses of these individuals to encountering Jesus we are left with the question – who is such a man who can provoke reactions like that in tough fishermen like Andrew and cynics like Nathanael? John, in his opening scene, has captured his readers' attention.

In chapter 3 we read of the Pharisee Nicodemus, who came to Jesus by night. His opening words also point to Jesus' Messiahship:

> Rabbi, we know you are a teacher who has come from God. For no one could perform the miraculous signs you are

doing if God were not with him (John 3:2).

The performing of signs and wonders was one of the criteria set out in the Old Testament for Messiah. Nicodemus (and others) recognised this. We do not hear much more of Nicodemus. He seems to have been a secret disciple. In John 7:50-51 he makes a half-hearted attempt to defend Jesus against his Pharisee colleagues but is shouted down. However, after the crucifixion, John 19:39 tells us that he was one of those who buried Jesus' body – a dangerous thing for someone in his position to do. So Nicodemus, like Andrew and the others, appears to have recognised Jesus as Messiah although he was perhaps not open about his views.

In John 4 we have the fascinating encounter with the woman at the well. The Lord Jesus breaks all social conventions by speaking to a woman – and a Samaritan woman at that - and asks her for a drink. As we read the incident we can trace the development in her understanding, and that of her friends.

- Are you greater than our father Jacob (verse 12)? The question implies that He could not possibly be.
- Sir, I can see that you are a prophet (verse 19). The fact that her life is an open book to Him has impressed and shaken her.
- I who speak to you am he (verse 26). Prompted by the woman's mention of Messiah in verse 25, Jesus confirms His identity to her.
- Come see a man who told me everything I ever did. Could this be the Christ (verse 29)? She is not entirely convinced, but is certainly open to the suggestion.
- We no longer believe just because of what you said; now we have heard for ourselves and we know that this man really is the Saviour of the world (verse 42). The Samaritans and the woman are now fully convinced. Interestingly, the Samaritans pick up a wider dimension to

the Lord's ministry than a narrow focus on Israel.

In his early chapters John has introduced us to a wide range of people who have recognised Jesus as Messiah, based on the fact that He displayed the attributes of Messiah that were predicted in the Old Testament. John's unspoken question echoes in our minds: 'That's what these people thought. What about you?'

The signs in the Gospel

John structures his Gospel around a series of signs and he presents these signs to demonstrate that 'Jesus is the Christ, the Son of God' (John 20:31). The Old Testament foretold that Messiah would perform signs and wonders and Jesus did this in order to demonstrate His credentials as Messiah.

After describing a particular incident, John sometimes adds a comment of his own, or reports a further dialogue which draws out the implications of what has just happened. For example in 2:11, after the water was turned into wine, John adds:

> This, the first of his miraculous signs, Jesus performed at Cana in Galilee. He thus revealed his glory, and his disciples put their faith in him.

Following the healing of the official's son, in 4:53-54, John concludes the incident by saying:

> He (the father) and all his household believed. This was the second miraculous sign that Jesus performed, having come from Judea to Galilee.

After the feeding of the five thousand we read:

> After the people saw the miraculous sign that Jesus did, they began to say, "Surely this is the Prophet who is to come into the world." (John 6:14)

In John 9 we have the fascinating incident of the healing of the man born blind. We can trace the growing confidence of the man, in the face of Pharisaic bullying, isolated from his parents who are cowed by the fear of the Jews and finally thrown out of the synagogue. At this point, the Lord seeks him out.

> When he found him he said, "Do you believe in the Son of Man?" "Who is he sir?" the man asked. "Tell me so that I may believe in him." Jesus said "You have now seen him; in fact, he is the one speaking with you." Then the man said, "Lord I believe." And he worshipped him. (John 9:35-38)

In these examples, we can see the implications – the disciples saw His glory and believed, the father and all his household believed, the people began to recognise Him and the formerly blind man not only accepted Him as Son of Man but worshipped Him (something that was only appropriate for God Himself.) That was how the people who saw the miraculous signs reacted... what do *we* make of the evidence?

The Lord's specific actions

In John 12:12-19 we read of the Lord riding into Jerusalem on a donkey. This is one action that He performed specifically to fulfil Zechariah's prophecy concerning Messiah. And in this incident it is the *kingship* of Messiah that is brought out. First, in verse 13, the crowd go out to meet him chanting:

> Blessed is he who comes in the name of the Lord! Blessed is the king of Israel!

Then in verses 14-15 John gives us the prophecy He is fulfilling:

> Do not be afraid, O Daughter of Zion; see, your king is coming, seated on a donkey's colt. (See Zechariah 9:9.)

John then sums up by describing how it was only later that the disciples understood the full implications of what they were seeing.

At first his disciples did not understand all this. Only after Jesus was glorified did they realise that these things had been written about him and that they had done these things to him. (John 12:16)

By a wide range of methods, then, John presents the Lord Jesus to us as the fulfiller of Israel's aspirations – recognised by those who encountered Him as the Christ, the Prophet, the Son of Man, the king of Israel, demonstrating the signs and wonders predicted of Messiah in the Old Testament scriptures. And finally, John describes the triumphant entry into Jerusalem, as Zechariah had promised Christ the king would do.

The Christ, the Messiah, was the focus of Jewish expectation. He was the One who had been foretold by the prophets who would come to deliver Israel, judge the nations, introduce justice on a worldwide basis, deliver the oppressed and establish a kingdom that would be 'everlasting.' In addition, he would offer Himself as a sacrifice for the sins of the people.

How could any man achieve all this? We are looking for a superman here. Or someone who was more than man: Someone who was God.

Jesus:
The Son
of God

Jesus: The Son of God

The previous section discussed the presentation by John of the Lord as 'The Christ' – the Messiah – the anointed one, predicted in the Old Testament as the coming Deliverer of Israel and fulfiller of all her aspirations.

But He was more than just a kind of 'local hero' for Israel because John also reveals Him as Son of God. In fact, a careful reading of the Old Testament predictions concerning Messiah indicates His divine nature.

However, as was indicated in the previous section, John's aim in writing his gospel was to demonstrate that Jesus was both 'the Christ,' and 'the Son of God' (John 30:31) and this section will explore John's revelation of the Lord Jesus as Son of God.

The Word: John 1

The opening verses of John's Gospel are profound.

> In the beginning was the Word, and the Word was with God, and the Word was God. He was with God in the beginning…. The Word became flesh and made his dwelling among us. (John 1:1-2, 14)

The word for 'Word' is the Greek *logos*, which is also used of the Lord Jesus in Revelation 19:13, where we read of the glorified Lord riding out in judgment against Satan and his hordes, treading "the winepress of the fury of the wrath of God Almighty" (Revelation 19:15).

John does not explain the term *logos,* from which we can infer that his readers knew what he meant. In fact there are two concepts of *logos*: The Jewish concept contained in the Old Testament, and the Gentile concept. *Logos* is used on a number of occasions in the Septuagint (the Greek translation of the Old Testament) and it describes the Word of God in action. For example:

in creation:

> By the word of the Lord were the heavens made, their starry host by the breath of his mouth. (Psalm 33:6)

in judgment:

> "Is not my word like fire," declares the Lord, "and like a hammer that breaks a rock in pieces?" (Jeremiah 23:29)

in the revelation of God's message:

> The word of the Lord came to me, saying… (Jeremiah 1:4)

To the Gentile philosophers *logos* was more of a guiding principle, a uniting force that formed the world and held the universe together, bringing stability and coherence to life and enlightenment and understanding to men.

John's approach is to bring the Jewish and Gentile ideas together: In John 1:3, we can see the *logos* in creation:

> Through him (the Word) all things were made; without him nothing was made that has been made.

From Genesis 1 we know that the world and all that is in it came into being by the spoken 'word' of God.

In the next verses of his gospel, John shows the *logos* bringing understanding and light to men and the revealer of God and his truth.

> In him was life, and that life was the light of men …. The true light that gives light to every man was coming into the world ….. For the law was given through Moses; grace and truth came through Jesus Christ. (John 1:4,9,17)

The high point of God's self-revelation up to that point had been the Law of Moses. But now we have grace and truth revealed through the *logos*, the Lord Jesus Christ.

However, it is important to notice that John does more than merely combine the Jewish and Greek ideas of *logos* – he extends in two ways, first by indicating that:

> The Word became flesh and made his dwelling among us.

The logos actually became flesh and blood and John and his companions had lived with Him, touched Him and ate with Him. No longer was He to be imagined as an impersonal force, like something from *Star Wars*.

Secondly, John declares Him as the perfect revelation of the invisible God, whom no one had seen at any time:

No one has even seen God, but God the One and Only, who is at the Father's side, has made him known. (John 1:18).

So the *logos* is personified in Christ and, although the coming of Jesus in human form took place in John's time, He, the *logos* had always existed. When we combine the information given to us in verses 1 and 18 we can see the foundation on which John is going to build his presentation of the divine Lord Jesus:

- The Word
- In the beginning
- With God; at the Father's side
- God; God the One and only
- The revealer of the invisible God.

Other New Testament passages echo these statements and indicate that the Lord Jesus fulfils other *logos* elements. For example Paul in Colossians 1:15-17 shows the Lord Jesus as:

- existing before creation
- the revealer of God

- the supreme Creator, and
- the sustainer of creation.

> He is the image of the invisible God, the firstborn over all creation. For by him all things were created … All things were created by him and for him. He is before all things, and in him all things hold together.

In Hebrews 1 also, we have the Lord Jesus presented as:

- the heir of creation
- the exact representation of God, and
- the sustainer of creation.

> In these last days he (God) has spoken to us by his Son, whom he appointed heir of all things, and through whom he made the universe. The Son is the radiance of God's glory and the exact representation of his being, sustaining all things by his powerful word. (Hebrews 1:2-3)

The way in which the Lord Jesus is presented to us in these passages shows that we are dealing with someone who is far more than the promised fulfiller of the political and religious aspirations of Israel. He is God Himself, who was with the Father in the beginning. Not only so, but He was the Creator and Sustainer of the universe and, in fact, everything was created not only *by* Him, but *for* Him. He came to reveal the Father and to give us the light of understanding. He was the *logos* that the Jewish scholars and Gentile philosophers groped for, but He came among us. Here we have God Himself: *Logos* made flesh: dwelling among us: revealing His glory.

But we are dealing with a profound mystery here: How can He be God and yet be 'with God?' How can He be 'the image' of One who is invisible? What is the relationship between Him and His Father?

The relationship with His Father

If He is the Son of God, how does the relationship with His Father show itself? This is a very complex subject but we'll look at a couple of aspects.

His identity with His Father

There are a number of places where the Lord Jesus is described as being the One who reveals the Father. The apostle John indicates that, although no one has ever seen God, Jesus Christ, 'who is at the Father's side, has made him known.' (John 1:18). In response to Philip's request to be shown the Father Jesus Himself stated:

> Don't you know me, Philip, even after I have been among you such a long time? Anyone who has seen me has seen the Father... Don't you believe that I am in the Father, and that the Father is in me? The words I say to you are not just my own. Rather, it is the Father, living in me, who is doing his work. (John 14:9-10)

This mutual indwelling is something that is hard for us to comprehend. Jesus is saying more here than simply that His acts are in harmony with what His Father would do if He were here. He is actually saying that the Father is doing the works through Him. As we see Jesus in action we see the Father in action. As we hear Jesus speak we hear the Father speak.

Doing the Father's work was, literally meat and drink to Him.

> "My food," said Jesus, "is to do the will of him who sent me and to finish his work." (John 4:34)

Perhaps the greatest aspect of this 'work' was the miracles He performed.

The miracles He did in His Father's name

As indicated earlier, John's Gospel is structured round the miraculous 'signs' that Jesus performed. In John 10, where we read of His discussion with the unbelieving Jews, Jesus again repeats that He was doing these miracles in His Father's name and that they should have recognised who He was from these miracles. The fact that they did not recognise His identity was proof that they were not His 'sheep.' He goes on

> My sheep listen to my voice; I know them, and they follow me. I give them eternal life, and they shall never perish; no-one can snatch them out of my hand. My Father, who has given them to me, is greater than all; no-one can snatch them out of my Father's hand. I and the Father are one. (John 10:27-30)

When we read these verses, we realise that this is more than man speaking. Yet we see again that the Lord Jesus is not autonomous in His actions. His sheep are protected in His hand, but beyond Him we have the Father, in whose hand they really are. He and His Father are one – a comment very similar to what He said to Philip earlier which means much more than that they are in agreement. The Father had direct involvement in all that was being done. And in verses 36-38 Jesus confirms that the fact that He did these miraculous signs demonstrated His deity.

> Why do you accuse me of blasphemy because I said, "I am God's Son"? Do not believe me unless I do what my Father does. But if I do it, even though you do not believe me, believe the miracles, that you may know and understand that the Father is in me and I in the Father.

The miraculous signs that Jesus did, then, were the Father's works, executed through Him. The signs demonstrated His power over nature, over illness and over death itself. But there were two particular powers that were delegated to the Son by the Father. These arguably were the greatest evidence of His deity.

The special powers delegated to Him by the Father

The Jews believed, and rightly so, that there were two powers, or rights that were exclusively God's – the right to judge man and the right to give eternal life. But when we come to John 5 we find that God the Father has delegated these powers to God the Son.

Jesus has just healed the lame man on the Sabbath and He justifies this by saying that His Father works every day, so He is doing the same. And in verse 18, we again get the Jews' hostile reaction to the Lord's suggestion that God is His own Father. But then the Lord Jesus raises the stakes even higher. In verse 19 He explains again that He does nothing on His own initiative, but only the works of His Father, who takes the Son into His confidence because of His love for Him. But the double bombshell comes in verses 21-23.

> For just as the Father raises the dead and gives them life, even so the Son gives life to whom he is pleased to give it. Moreover, the Father judges no one, but has entrusted all judgment to the Son, that all may honour the Son just as they honour the Father. He who does not honour the Son does not honour the Father, who sent him.

Here we see these twin powers of deity – the right to judge mankind and the right to bestow eternal life – being given to the Lord Jesus by His Father. We know that Jesus raised people back to natural life on two occasions at least – the widow's son in Luke 7 and Lazarus in John 11. But here He is speaking of eternal, imperishable life, the life of God Himself. And just in case we have not appreciated the full impact of this, He explains in verses 25-28:

> I tell you the truth, a time is coming and has now come when the dead will hear the voice of the Son of God and those who hear will live. For as the Father has life in himself, so he has granted the Son to have life in himself... Do not be amazed at this, for a time is coming when all who are in their graves will hear his voice and come out...'

What sort of person would say such things? For someone who is nothing more than man it would be completely insane. But the Lord Jesus was not insane. He was proclaiming His deity. What does

He mean by 'life in himself'? This is more than the life *we* possess. It is the self-sustaining, self-perpetuating life of God. We see a suggestion of this in John's introduction of the Lord Jesus to us at the start of his Gospel.

> In him was life, and that life was the light of men. (John 1:4)

John is saying more than the fact that He was alive. He is in fact the source of life and we see that life presented to us as it affects mankind. Because the glorious truth is that the Lord Jesus not only possesses that life, but is willing to give that life to those who follow Him.

> I tell you the truth, whoever hears my word and believes him who sent me has eternal life and will not be condemned; he has crossed over from death to life. (John 5:24)

The Lord Jesus possesses that life that is the light of men. But that self-sustaining life was granted to Him by the Father (verse 26). The Lord never operated independently. He always stood in relation with His Father. During His earthly ministry He was always the Son – Son of God and Son of Man. So committed was He to doing the Father's works and revealing Him that seeing Him is seeing the Father.

But it is not only in the granting of eternal life, that the Son possesses this power of deity, because the task of judging has also been committed to Him. In John 5:22 we read that the Father judges no one, but has committed all judging to the Son. In this chapter there are two reasons why judgment has been entrusted to the Son. Firstly, in 23 we read that it is in order that all may honour the Son as they honour the Father. It is not possible to honour the one without honouring the other, which is only to be expected, given that the Lord Jesus is "the exact representation of his being" (Hebrews 1:3).

Secondly, in John 5:27 we read that:

He (the Father) has given him (the Son) authority to judge because he is the Son of Man.

As we noted earlier, Jesus' application of this title to Himself is based on Daniel 7:13-14, where the prophet has a vision of 'one like a son of man' who has authority over all nations and peoples of every language – in other words, the establishment of His kingdom on the earth.

But it is important to realise that the judgment of mankind will be executed by One who has lived as man, enduring all the pressures, temptations and trials that befall all of us. He understands the difficulties people face, therefore He is the One to judge.

There is one final aspect of deity to be considered in this brief review and that is the instances where the Lord Jesus takes on the title – I AM: which was the name by which God introduced Himself to Moses.

The use of the term 'I AM'

In John 8, we read of a discussion between the Lord Jesus and the Jews about Abraham. The discussion ends with Jesus stating that Abraham rejoiced at the thought of Jesus' day (i.e. His coming to earth). The Jews were scathing:

> "You are not yet fifty years old," the Jews said to him, "and you have seen Abraham!" "I tell you the truth," Jesus answered, "Before Abraham was born, I am!" (John 8:57-58)

The response of the Jews was to pick up stones to stone Him for blasphemy. But what, exactly, was he claiming here? It does not even appear to make sense grammatically. And why did the Jews want to stone Him? Just for saying that He was older than Abraham?

The words Jesus uses for 'I am' in this passage (*ego eimi*), are the words used in the Septuagint by God to reveal Himself. For example, in Isaiah 41:4:

Who has done this and carried it through, calling forth the generations from the beginning? I, the Lord – with the first of them and with the last – I am he (*ego eimi*)

Similarly in Isaiah 43:10-11 we read:

"You are my witnesses," declares the Lord, "and my servant whom I have chosen, so that you may know and believe me and understand that I am he (*ego eimi)*. Before me no god was formed, nor will there be one after me. I, even I, am the Lord, and apart from me there is no saviour."

The aim of both passages is to demonstrate the exclusiveness of the God of Israel; He is there from beginning to end (reminiscent of Revelation 1:8). He alone is God; He alone is Saviour. And in both these passages, among others, He uses the *ego eimi* formula to draw attention to Himself in the strongest way.

The same words are used in Exodus 3:14, when the Lord introduces Himself to Moses.

> God said to Moses, "I AM WHO I AM" (*ego eimi ho on*). This is what you are to say to the Israelites: I AM (*ho on*) has sent me to you.

In John's Gospel *ego eimi* is used in a number of settings. It is used by the formerly blind man in 9:9 to confirm strongly his identity. Jesus also uses the phrase in more than one context. Like the blind man He uses it to identify Himself – e.g. to the disciples in John 6:20 where we read of Him walking on the water in the storm and to those who came to arrest Him in John 18:5,6. In these three passages the *NIV* adds additional words to *ego eimi* to convey the sense of the passage:

- John 9:9: I am *he.*
- John 6:20: *It is I.*
- John 18:5,6: I am *he.*

Thus, although, on occasion, *ego eimi* is used by an ordinary man, when we look at the passages that place the phrase in the mouth of Jesus, we see something more than just a simple matter of identification. In John 6 He is walking on the water – not something that an 'ordinary' person would do and in John 18, the apostle tells us that when He said '*Ego eimi*' the reaction of the guards who came to arrest Him was to draw back and fall to the ground. This is not the normal response of soldiers who come to arrest an unarmed man.

John, by reporting these events in this way, tries to draw our attention to this man. He is using the language of deity and the context and the reactions of those present, indicate that there is something quite out of the ordinary going on.

Jesus also uses *ego eimi* to describe different aspects of His role in God's purposes. The 'I ams' of Jesus are famous – I am the bread of life (John 6:35, 48); I am the good shepherd (John 10:11); I am the way, the truth and the life (John 14:6). But again, when we look at the truth He is trying to get across in these situations, we can see that this is no mere man talking:

I am the bread of life... here is the bread that comes down from heaven, which a man may eat and not die. I am the living bread that came down from heaven. If anyone eats of this bread, he will live forever. This bread is my flesh, which I will give for the life of the world. (John 6:48-51)

I am the good shepherd. The good shepherd lays down his life for the sheep ... I know my sheep and my sheep know me – just as the Father knows me and I know the Father – and I lay down my life for the sheep... The reason my Father loves me is that I lay down my life – only to take it up again... I have authority to lay it down and authority to take it up again. This command I received from my Father. (John 10:11-18)

Jesus answered "I am the way, the truth and the life. No-one comes to the Father except through me. If you really knew me, you would know my Father as well…. Anyone who has seen me has seen the Father…Don't you believe that I am in the Father and that the Father is in me? The words I say to you are not just my own. Rather, it is the Father, living in me, who is doing his work." (John 14:6-10)

When we see the context of these occurrences of *ego eimi* and appreciate what Jesus is saying here, we soon realise that no man in his right mind would say these things. Here is someone who claims to be 'bread from heaven' that gives eternal life to those who 'eat' of Him. He willingly gives up His life for His 'sheep' – in fact, for the world. But more than that, He has authority not only to lay down His life, but to take it up again. This authority was given to Him by the Father. Indeed, there is a complete identification of Himself with the Father here – if we want to know the Father, get to know *Him*; if we want to see the Father, look at *Him*; if we want to hear the Father, listen to *Him*. And as He makes these astonishing claims for Himself, He does so with the *ego eimi* formula that the God of Israel used to reveal Himself to His people. The Lord Jesus' entire message is shot through with revelations of His identity as God. It is woven into the cloth of what He is saying and it's impossible to understand His teaching without taking this on board.

The Jewish people to whom the Lord spoke in John 8 were well aware of the implications of His use of that emphatic language and that was why they picked up the stones. The tragedy was that they did not accept His words, and in rejecting Him, condemned their nation to centuries of hardship.

In conclusion…

By now we are a long way away from the Lord Jesus as 'great teacher', or a 'good man' or even 'the great deliverer of Israel.' We are now in the realms of God Himself. His claims are stupendous. As C S Lewis observes, for anyone to make such claims for himself he must be either supremely evil, or completely insane ... or else He must be telling the truth.

Many have asserted that Jesus never claimed to be the Son of God and that this was an error made by the early Christians. However, when we look at John's account of the Lord's teaching, it is impossible to escape the fact that:

- He was absolutely clear of His identity as Son of God
- It is impossible to understand His mission without realising His identity as Son of God
- If we regard Him only as an inspired teacher how can we take on board His words on:

  o His relationship to God the Father
  o The equal honouring of both Father and Son
  o The granting of eternal life
  o The power to judge

o His willingness to take to Himself the title of God that epitomises His eternal existence.

He is the Alpha and the Omega: The beginning and the end. He was there in the beginning. In fact everything was created by Him and for Him. He will be there at the end: He is the heir of all things.

And He is our Lord.

Jesus:
Man and God

Jesus: Man and God

Who is Jesus?

We know that the Lord Jesus, after asking the disciples who others thought Him to be, turned to them and asked them directly who *they* thought He was. Similarly we should answer that question ourselves. Who do you think Jesus is? Who do I think He is?

Man and God

In his first letter to Timothy Paul wrote:

> For there is one God and one mediator between God and men, *the man Christ Jesus*, who gave himself as a ransom for all men. (1 Timothy 2:5-6)

Jesus existed and was most definitely a man. He was conceived by a woman in a unique miraculous way. The angel told his mother to be:

> "The Holy Spirit will come upon you, and the power of the Most High will overshadow you. So the holy one to be born will be called the Son of God." (Luke 1:35)

And, as we have seen, the title 'Son of God' implies deity. We may have problems associating 'Son of God' with 'God' but not the Jews of His day. One of the most sceptical was Thomas. Following Christ's resurrection we read:

> Now Thomas (called Didymus), one of the Twelve, was not with the disciples when Jesus came. So the other disciples told him, "We have seen the Lord!" But he said to them, "Unless I see the nail marks in his hands and put my finger where the nails were, and put my hand into his side, I will not believe it." A week later his disciples were in the house again, and Thomas was with them. Though the doors were locked,

Jesus came and stood among them and said, "Peace be with you!" Then he said to Thomas, "Put your finger here; see my hands. Reach out your hand and put it into my side. Stop doubting and believe." Thomas said to him, "My Lord and *my God*!" (John 20:24-28)

Paul also stated this when he wrote to Timothy that "God was manifest in the flesh" (1 Timothy 3:16; KJV). The *NIV*, going with an alternative reading, has:

Beyond all question, the mystery of godliness is great: He appeared in a body.

But the 'he' must refer to God for two reasons; (1) 'God' is the nearest noun for the pronoun 'he' to be linked with – see verse 15; (2) it is hardly a great mystery if a man appeared in a body! We all do!

Then and now

It is true to say that many today struggle with the view that Jesus is God manifest in the flesh. However, as we have seen earlier in this publication, this was the clear implication of what He taught and did. So obvious was this that the Jews who did not believe in Him attempted to stone Him for blasphemy.

When the truth concerning Jesus spread wider, it is interesting to note that people did not deny His deity; rather it was his humanity that some had trouble with. It was clear to them that Jesus was God, but how could the holy God inhabit sinful flesh. Thus their theology detracted from the humanity of Christ, believing Him not to have a real body but only the appearance of one. John deals with this error in two of his letters.

> Many deceivers, who do not acknowledge Jesus Christ as coming in the flesh, have gone out into the world. Any such person is the deceiver and the antichrist. (2 John 7)

This is how you can recognize the Spirit of God: Every spirit that acknowledges that Jesus Christ has come in the flesh is from God, but every spirit that does not acknowledge Jesus is not from God. This is the spirit of the antichrist, which you have heard is coming and even now is already in the world. (1 John 4:2-3)

This was part of the teaching of people called the Gnostics. By denying that Jesus was truly human they were, in fact, denying His literal death and resurrection. He only 'appeared' to have a human body, thus he only 'appeared' to die on the cross, and only 'appeared' to be raised from the dead. If they were right, the wages of sin – death – was not paid by Christ.

Similarly today if people deny that Jesus is the creator God, the gospel is deficient. Redemption requires payment of equal or greater worth than that which is to be redeemed. Paul wrote:

For the creation was subjected to frustration, not by its own choice, but by the will of the one who subjected it, in hope that the creation itself will be liberated from its bondage to decay and brought into the glorious freedom of the children of God. We know that the whole creation has been groaning as in the pains of childbirth right up to the present time. (Romans 8:20-22)

The only One of equal or greater worth than the whole creation, and all who have lived and will live, can only be the Creator Himself. Christ must be that Creator and if He is not, our faith is futile and we are still in our sins.

Jesus and Paul

Undoubtedly Paul had heard the teaching that Jesus was the Christ (the promised Messiah) and was the Son of God (God manifest in the flesh). It was such teaching as this which fuelled his fury against those Jews who believed such truths and taught them to others. He imprisoned them and saw them stoned to death. However, outside of Damascus that all changed, and after that what did Paul teach about Jesus?

Saul spent several days with the disciples in Damascus. At once he began to preach in the synagogues that *Jesus is the Son of God*. All those who heard him were astonished and asked, "Isn't he the man who caused havoc in Jerusalem among those who call on this name? And hasn't he come here to take them as prisoners to the chief priests?" Yet Saul grew more and more powerful and baffled the Jews living in Damascus by proving that *Jesus is the Christ*. (Acts 9:19-22)

This echoes the teaching of John's Gospel (John 20:30-31) and we see this repeated throughout the Acts as Paul visited different groups of Jews. In some of his later letters, written to Gentiles, he is even more explicit. Consider the following three passages:

Ephesians 1:19-23

That power is like the working of his mighty strength, which he exerted in Christ when he raised him from the dead and seated him at his right hand in the heavenly realms, far above all rule and authority, power and dominion, and every title that can be given, not only in the present age but also in the one to come. And God placed all things under his feet and appointed him to be head over everything for the church, which is his body, the fullness of him who fills everything in every way.

Philippians 2:6-11

Who, being in very nature God, did not consider equality with God something to be grasped, but made himself nothing, taking the very nature of a servant, being made in human likeness. And being found in appearance as a man, he humbled himself and became obedient to death - even death on a cross! Therefore God exalted him to the highest place and gave him the name that is above every name, that at the name of Jesus every knee should bow, in heaven and on earth and under the earth, and every tongue confess that Jesus Christ is Lord, to the glory of God the Father.

Colossians 1:15-19

He is the image of the invisible God, the firstborn over all creation. For by him all things were created: things in heaven and on earth, visible and invisible, whether thrones or powers or rulers or authorities; all things were created by him and for him. He is before all things, and in him all things hold together. And he is the head of the body, the church; he is the beginning and the firstborn from among the dead, so that in everything he might have the supremacy. For God was pleased to have all his fullness dwell in him.

In the passage from Philippians we see Christ is "in very nature God". However, He did not consider equality with God something to be "grasped" or "kept hold of". In other words He was prepared to give up certain things, like His glory and some aspects of knowledge, to become a man and so take on death. However, it is the

Colossians passage we wish to consider in more detail.

Colossians 1:15-19

Here Jesus is called "the image of the invisible God". In Hebrews 1:3 the *KJV* version has "the express image" of God, whereas the *NIV* has "the exact representation". This is who Jesus is, "the exact representation of God". When Philip wanted to see the Father, Christ said, "Anyone who has seen me has seen the Father" (John 14:9). And earlier the Lord had said:

> "I tell you the truth, the Son can do nothing by himself; he can do only what he sees his Father doing, because whatever the Father does the Son also does. For the Father loves the Son and shows him all he does … For just as the Father raises the dead and gives them life, even so the Son gives life to whom he is pleased to give it. Moreover, the Father judges no one, but has entrusted all judgment to the Son, that all may honour the Son just as they honour the Father. He

who does not honour the Son does not honour the Father, who sent him. "I tell you the truth, whoever hears my word and believes him who sent me has eternal life and will not be condemned; he has crossed over from death to life … For as the Father has life in himself, so he has granted the Son to have life in himself. And he has given him authority to judge because he is the Son of Man." (John 5:19-27)

Jesus is also called "the firstborn over all creation". Here the *KJV* has "the firstborn of every creature" and because of this some say that Jesus was the first being God created. However the word 'firstborn' has nothing to do with either being the first in time or with being born. It is a term of pre-eminence, as such expressions as Prime Minister or Archbishop, and this is clear from later in the passage where we read that the Lord is called "the firstborn from among the dead". However, He was most certainly not the first person raised from the dead as He, himself, raised a number of people, including Lazarus. However, we do not have forgiveness of sins because Lazarus died, and neither do we have justification because he was brought back to life. However, Christ's death and resurrections achieved both: "He was delivered over to death for our sins and was raised to life for our justification" (Romans 4:25). As such Christ is the pre-eminent One raised from the dead; i.e. He is the firstborn from the dead. Christ is also the pre-eminent One over all creation. Why?

> For by him all things were created: things in heaven and on earth, visible and invisible, whether thrones or powers or rulers or authorities; all things were created by him and for him. He is before all things, and in him all things hold together. (Colossians 1:16-17)

Thus Christ is the creator, and this is how John introduces Him in the opening words of his gospel.

> In the beginning was the Word, and the Word was with God, and the Word was God. He was with God in the beginning.

Through him all things were made; without him nothing was made that has been made. (John 1:1-3)

Thus Christ created all things and holds all things together. He is the One who loves His creation and He is the One who died for people's sins, and conquered sin and death so that He might justify them. Because of all this, and more, Paul wrote:

.... so that in everything he might have the supremacy.
(Colossians 1:18)

Jesus: to you and me

So if the Lord Jesus asked you the question "Who do you say that I am?" what would be your answer? If he asked me, I would side with Thomas and say ...

My Lord and my God.

More on Jesus

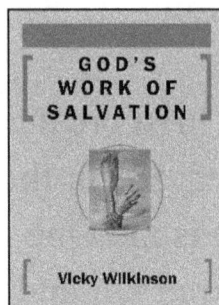

Put on the Lord Jesus Christ
By Vicky Wilkinson

The Deity of Christ
By Vicky Wilkinson

God's Work of Salvation
By Vicky Wilkinson

For details of these books please visit

www.obt.org.uk

They can be ordered from that website or from:

The Open Bible Trust,
Fordland Mount, Upper Basildon,
Reading, RG8 8LU, UK.

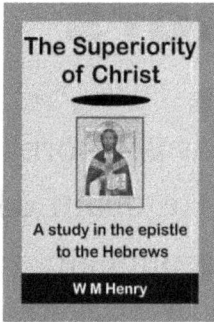
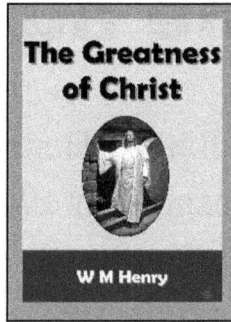
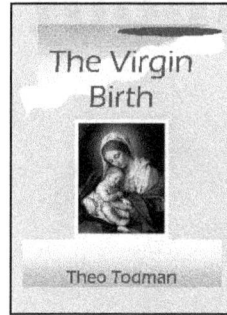

The Superiority of Christ
A study in the epistle to the Hebrews
By W M Henry

The Greatness of Christ
By W M Henry

The Virgin Birth
By Theo Todman

****

All these books are also available as eBooks
from Amazon and Apple
and as KDP paperbacks from Amazon.

About the authors

William Henry was born in Glasgow in 1949. He qualified as a Chartered Accountant and worked in the accountancy profession before entering academia, where he spent 25 years in teaching and research. At present he is an education consultant working with undergraduate and postgraduate students. He lives in Glasgow with his wife and two daughters. He is an international speaker and has spoken in Canada, Australia and the Netherlands.

Michael Penny was born in Ebbw Vale, Gwent, Wales in 1943. He read Mathematics at the University of Reading, before teaching for twelve years and becoming the Director of Mathematics and Business Studies at Queen Mary's College Basingstoke in Hampshire, England. In 1978 he entered Christian publishing, and in 1984 became the administrator of The Open Bible Trust.

He held this position for seven years, before moving to the USA and becoming pastor of Grace Church in New Berlin, Wisconsin. He returned to Britain in 1999, and is at present the Administrator and Editor of The Open Bible Trust. In 2010 he was elected Chairman of Churches Together in Reading, where he speaks in a number of churches of different denominations. He is also a member of the Advisory Committee to Reading University Christian Union and is senior chaplain at Reading College. He lives near Reading with his wife and has appeared on Premier Radio and BBC Radio Berkshire many times. He has made several speaking tours of America, Canada, Australia, New Zealand and the Netherlands, as well as others to South Africa and the Philippines. Some of his writings have been translated into German and Russian.

Search magazine

Michael Penny is editor of *Search* magazine and
W M Henry is a regular contributor

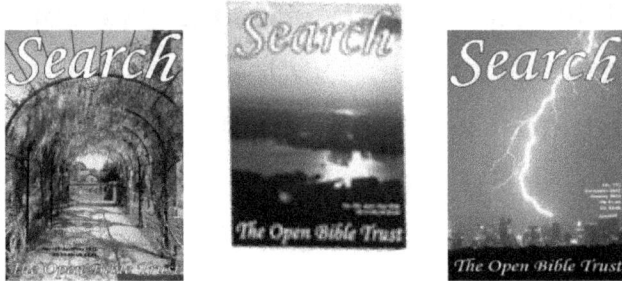

For a free sample of The Open Bible Trust's
magazine Search, please email

admin@obt.org.uk

or visit

www.obt.org.uk/search

****

Both authors have written many publications
details of these can be seen at

www.obt.org.uk/william-henry

www.obt.org.uk/michael-penny

Also by W M Henry and Michael Penny

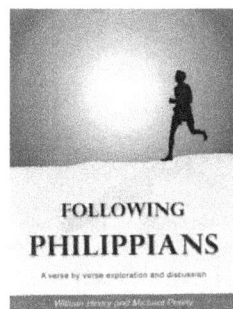

The Will of God
Past and Present
In the Bible & the 21st Century
William Henry and Michael Penny

Sit! Walk! Stand!
The Christian life in Ephesians
William Henry and Michael Penny

FOLLOWING PHILIPPIANS
A verse by verse exploration and discussion
William Henry and Michael Penny

For details of these books please visit

www.obt.org.uk

They can be ordered from that website or from:

The Open Bible Trust,
Fordland Mount, Upper Basildon,
Reading, RG8 8LU, UK.

All these books are also available as eBooks
from Amazon and Apple
and as KDP paperbacks from Amazon.

About this book

Who is Jesus?

In Matthew 16:13-16 the Lord asked the disciples who the people said He was. What were their answers? Some answers were understandable, with a grain of truth, but none were correct. Then He turned to His disciples and asked them. What was their answer?

And what about today? Who do people, today, say Jesus is? Again, some of the answers from the man in the street may have a grain of truth, but how many people really know and appreciate who Jesus is? Do you? Who do you say that He is? What is your answer?

Publications of The Open Bible Trust must be in accordance with its evangelical, fundamental and dispensational basis. However, beyond this minimum, writers are free to express whatever beliefs they may have as their own understanding, provided that the aim in so doing is to further the object of The Open Bible Trust. A copy of the doctrinal basis is available at

www.obt.org.uk/doctrinal-basis

or from:

THE OPEN BIBLE TRUST
Fordland Mount, Upper Basildon,
Reading, RG8 8LU, GB

www.ingramcontent.com/pod-product-compliance
Lightning Source LLC
Chambersburg PA
CBHW070541030426
42337CB00016B/2302